Cryptocurrency

Investing and Trading in the Blockchain. Bitcoin, Ethereum, Litecoin, IOTA, Ripple, Dash, Monero, Neo & More!

Sean Duncan

CONTENTS

Introduction

The last two years have seen growing public and media interest in Bitcoin and other popular cryptocurrencies. This has been mainly fueled by the rapid rise in value of the major cryptocurrencies in the recent period of time. The soaring prices have turned cryptocurrency investors into overnight millionaires and billionaires. Consider this: if you bought one Bitcoin at $1000 in January 2017 and left it untouched, you'd have $17000 by early December 2017. That's a 1700% profit!

The supernormal profits being made in the cryptocurrency market have caught the attention of the public, and everyone wants to get involved and make themselves a fortune. However, the cryptocurrency market is not without its risks. If you want to make money in cryptocurrencies, you need to have a good understanding of the technology behind it, and how it could be implemented in our future. This book is a comprehensive guide into cryptocurrencies. It will inform you of the basics in how to start investing and making money in the cryptocurrency market.

Chapter One:

An Introduction to Cryptocurrency

O n the 22nd of May, 2010, a Florida developer named Laszlo Hanyecz got his name into history books when he ordered two pepperoni pizzas. There wasn't anything really special about the pizzas. The transaction got into the books of history because of the mode of payment Laszlo used to pay for the meal. Laszlo paid 10,000 Bitcoins for the two pizzas, making this the first transaction where a cryptocurrency was used to pay for a real word commodity. Back then, cryptocurrencies were virtually unknown. One Bitcoin was worth just a few cents at the time. Had Laszlo chosen to keep his Bitcoins and forego the pizzas, his Bitcoins would have been worth over 190 million dollars today!

Seven years since Laszlo's historical transaction, cryptocurrencies have become a global phenomenon. While most people do not understand the technical aspects of cryptocurrencies, everyone is talking about them. This book will take you into the geeky world of cryptocurrencies and help you understand how they work and how you can make money with them. However, we first need to answer the following question, 'What is a cryptocurrency?'

The term cryptocurrency refers to any digital medium of exchange that is based on cryptography and encryption. Cryptocurrencies rely on the rules of mathematics to regulate the production of new units, ensure security and prevent fraud. The term cryptocurrency is a mash up of the words cryptography and currency. To break it down further, a cryptocurrency is simply a set of entries in a digital database which can only be changed once specific conditions are fulfilled. Each unit of a given cryptocurrency is referred to as a token or a coin.

Since cryptocurrencies are digital in nature, they cannot be printed by the government as is the case with ordinary currency. So, where do they come from? Before we get to how they are produced, we first need to take a deeper look into how they work. I mentioned that cryptocurrencies rely on the rules of mathematics. Before any cryptocurrency transaction can be completed, it has to be verified by a network of computers. These computers verify the transaction by solving complex mathematical equations in a process known as mining. By verifying transactions, this network of computers keeps the whole system running. In return, the system creates and awards new coins to the computers in the network after a predetermined number of transactions.

One thing that totally sets cryptocurrencies apart from ordinary currencies is that they are not backed or regulated by any bank, government or central authority. To ensure accountability, cryptocurrencies rely on a non-trust based public system known as the blockchain, (I will discuss this in greater detail in the next chapter) to record and verify transactions.

History of Cryptocurrencies

To most people, cryptocurrencies are a fairly recent phenomenon. Before the advent of Bitcoin in 2009, cryptocurrencies were virtually unheard of. However, attempts at creating a digital payment system started long ago. The seemingly new phenomenon we are seeing today is actually a result of decades of painstaking mathematical research and strong-gut attempts by progressive thinking mathematicians and developers.

The first recorded attempt at storing value in something other than cash happened in the 1980's and came as a result of necessity. Noticing the huge amount of money in the oil industry, bandits started raiding petrol stations in remote areas of the Netherlands for cash. Unfortunately, the petrol stations could not close at night since trucks needed to refuel. To keep the bandits at bay, someone came up with the idea of putting money into smartcards, giving birth to electronic money. Instead of carrying cash, drivers were issued these smart cards, which they could then use to refuel at petrol stations.

At about the same time, an American cryptographer named David Chaum was investigating different ways of creating electronic cash. One of his major concerns was that electronic cash had to be similar to ordinary cash in that it would allow people to make hand-to-hand transactions safely and privately. Improving on the RSA algorithm which had been invented in 1977, Chaum came up with a blinding formula which allowed the secure exchange of unalterable information. Chaum moved to the Netherlands – then a hotbed of mathematics and cryptography research – where he teamed up with other cryptocurrency enthusiasts to create Digicash, the first internet money invention. Just like ordinary currency, the supply and use of this digital cash was controlled by Chaum's company.

The invention of Chaum's blinded cash was very innovative, and as a result, it received a lot of press attention. The press attention brought along very exciting deals for Digicash, with Deutsche Bank, Microsoft and other big corporations interested in partnering with Digicash. However, after making a series of missteps and falling foul with the Netherlands Central Bank, Digicash ended up in bankruptcy in 1998.

Following the hype of Chaum's Digicash, many other startup companies became interested in digital currencies. In 1996, an amateur economic history scholar named Douglas Jackson came up with E-gold, an online platform that gave people gold-credits (e-gold) in exchange for physical gold deposits. E-gold was driven by Jackson's notion that since his virtual currency was backed by gold, it would be stronger than fiat currencies, which are not backed by any physical asset. E-gold gained a lot of popularity. By 2005, the platform had over 3.5 million users in 165 countries. Unfortunately, E-gold's popularity attracted a lot of criminals, and as a result, it was shut down by the FBI in 2005.

In 1997, a British cryptographer known as Adam Back came up with the 'hashcash' proof of work algorithm that would become the foundation on which modern-day cryptocurrencies are built on. Back's algorithm inspired the system that modern day cryptocurrencies use to mine new coins. In 1998, a Computer Science graduate named Wei Dai outlined the working of a virtual currency known as b-money. In his white paper, Wei Dai proposed many of the features associated with modern-day cryptocurrency, including anonymity and decentralization. However, Dai did not implement b-money.

Still searching for a viable form of virtual cash, a software company known as Confinity came up with a system that allowed people to make payments via email. Soon after, they focused their attention on allowing people to pay eBay sellers through email, giving birth to PayPal. PayPal gained massive success and grew to become the largest player in online payments.

In October 2008, a person or group of persons using the pseudonym Satoshi Nakamoto introduced Bitcoin, the first modern-day cryptocurrency. In 2009, Satoshi mined the first block of Bitcoin, giving rise to a digital currency that was both secure and free from regulation by any central authority. Bitcoin was also the first cryptocurrency to apply the concept of the blockchain. Following the success of Bitcoin and blockchain technology, several other programmers and cryptographers started creating their own cryptocurrencies. In April 2011, Vincent Durham created Namecoin, which added some innovative features to Bitcoin's infrastructure. In 2012, Ripple was created, functioning both as a cryptocurrency and as an electronic platform for financial transactions. Peercoin was also launched in 2012, introducing a new proof of stake security method. Currently, there are over 1500 cryptocurrencies in the world, whose combined market capitalization is over $600 billion.

Attributes of A Cryptocurrency

Cryptocurrencies have certain attributes that set them apart from fiat currencies. These include:

Anonymity: This attribute is one of the reasons behind the popularity of cryptocurrencies. Cryptocurrency wallet addresses are not linked to a person's name or physical address. This allows cryptocurrency users to make transactions without having to reveal their identity.

Transparency: Cryptocurrencies use a non-trust based system which relies on transparency. Every single cryptocurrency transaction is recorded in a huge digital ledger. The information within this ledger is publicly accessible to all the computers in the network. This means that anyone can see all the transactions and the number of coins owned by every cryptocurrency address. Despite this transparency, the addresses cannot be used to identify the owner of the coins.

Decentralization: One of the most revolutionary attributes of cryptocurrencies is that they are not regulated or controlled by any central entity. Instead, cryptocurrencies operate on a devolved system where the processing and validation of transactions is done by all the computers within the network. Due to their decentralized nature, no government or financial central authority can influence cryptocurrencies. Their decentralized nature also means that cryptocurrencies are always active. If some of the computers in the network go offline, others simply step in to fill the gap.

Speed: Another attribute that has contributed to the massive uptake of cryptocurrencies is their transaction speed. It only takes a couple of minutes for the computers in the network to verify a cryptocurrency transaction, allowing you to instantly send money to any part of the world. Compare this to banks which need several days to process and confirm transactions.

Ease of setting up: Getting started with cryptocurrencies is a breeze. There are no checks. Simply set up a cryptocurrency wallet in a few minutes and you are good to go.

Compare this to banks, which require you to go through a number of checks before you can create a bank account.

Irreversibility: Unlike regular money transactions, cryptocurrencies do not have chargebacks. Once a transaction is completed, it cannot be reversed.

Advantages of Cryptocurrency

The massive uptake and popularity of cryptocurrencies in recent years has been driven by the distinct advantages offered by cryptocurrencies. Some of these advantages include:

Instant Funds Transfer

One of the inconveniences of banks and regular payment processing systems is that it usually takes several days to process and confirm payments. Cryptocurrencies get rid of this inconvenience by allowing you to transfer funds anywhere in the world within a matter of minutes. The same case applies with credit card payments. If your business accepts credit card payments, you are forced to wait for several days before the money gets to your bank account. With cryptocurrency payments, the funds are accessible and ready to be used immediately once the transaction is completed.

Fraud Protection

One of the major challenges faced by online businesses is the risk of fraud. Many credit card fraudsters buy items online and then later on claim chargebacks, which leads to losses for online businesses. With cryptocurrency payments, businesses are protected from such fraudsters since cryptocurrency transactions are irreversible. Cryptocurrency transactions have to be validated by the entire network before the transaction is completed, thereby eliminating the risk of counterfeit payments. By paying for goods using cryptocurrency, customers also keep their financial information safe from hackers who usually target small businesses.

Privacy

One of the attributes of a cryptocurrency is that it has to offer anonymity. By not linking personally identifiable information to your cryptocurrency wallet, you are able to exchange money with other people without revealing your identity. This is important when you want to keep your transactions away from prying eyes.

Global Access

A huge part of the population in remote areas of the world do not have access to banks and financial institutions. However, most of the population in these areas have access to internet linked mobile devices. The number of mobile phone users is set to exceed 4.7 billion in early 2018. A large chunk of this population depends on mobile devices for their financial transactions. Cryptocurrency gives this population the opportunity to save their money and make financial transactions on their own terms.

Total Control Over Your Funds

One of the disadvantages of a payment system that is controlled by a central authority is that you are never in full control of your account and funds. The bank or company has the final say over your account and funds. For instance, you have no control over your PayPal account. If PayPal feels that you are not acting in compliance with their terms and conditions, they have the power to freeze your funds without even consulting you. With cryptocurrency, no one wields such power over your funds. You have total ownership and control over your funds. No one has access to your wallet's private key, which means that no one can mess around with your money.

Low Transaction Fees

Another disadvantage of banks and conventional payment processing companies is that every transaction is accompanied by processing fees. With cryptocurrency, there are no third parties, which means that you can make transactions at absolutely no fee. However, due to the technical nature of cryptocurrency, many users rely on third parties to maintain their wallets. These third parties will definitely charge a fee for their fees, though their fees are nowhere near as high as what banks will charge you.

Are Cryptocurrencies Real Money?

Ever since Bitcoin was first introduced to the world, there has been a raging debate as to whether cryptocurrencies qualify to be referred to as money. The back and fourth argument has attracted support from big players in the cryptocurrency and financial industries. Just recently, the CEO and Chairman of JPMorgan Chase referred to Bitcoin as a fraud. But is this really true? Are cryptocurrencies really money? To answer this question, we need to understand what money is. Money is defined by the following properties:

Uniformity: For something to be termed as money, each unit of measure should have similar purchasing unit to another equal unit of measure. For example, one dollar has similar purchasing power to another dollar.

Portability: For something to be used as money, it should be easy to carry and transfer to others. For instance, you cannot use a sack of potatoes or a goat as money because you cannot easily carry them.

Divisibility: Money should be able to be divided into smaller units without loss of value. For instance, using the example above, you cannot divide the goat into smaller units without loss of value.

Durability: Money should be capable of withstanding repeated use – repeated exchange between people, storage in pockets and wallets, wear and tear, etc.

Acceptability: Something can only function as money if it widely accepted as a means of exchange.

Fungibility: This means that a unit of money should be essentially interchangeable with another similar unit without profit or loss. This means that one unit of money should not be superior to a similar unit. For instance, a ten dollar bill can be exchanged with another ten dollar bill without gain or loss.

Based on the above properties of money, we can now deduce whether cryptocurrencies meet the requirements of money. Cryptocurrencies are uniform, since each unit of cryptocurrency has similar purchasing power to another equal unit of the same cryptocurrency. Since cryptocurrencies exist digitally, they are extremely portable. They have no weight and size restrictions. You can store them online, on your computer or on your smartphone. Transferring them to others is easy and frictionless. Compare this to paper money, which is cumbersome and dangerous to carry around in large quantities.

Cryptocurrencies have high divisibility, with most being capable of division up to 8 decimal places. Despite not having the same level of acceptance as fiat money, it is steadily growing. Currently, there are over 35 million active cryptocurrency wallets. Hundreds of thousands of businesses also accept cryptocurrency payments. Considering that cryptocurrency is still in its infancy stage, their acceptance will only keep growing.

Cryptocurrencies are digital entries that do not exist physically. This means that they don't face the risk of physical degradation. Cryptocurrencies cannot be destroyed as happens with paper money. So as long as you have your wallet password and you keep it safe, you cannot lose your cryptocurrencies. Finally, cryptocurrencies are highly fungible. You can interchange a unit of cryptocurrency for another similar unit without gain or loss. Based on the above properties, it becomes evident that cryptocurrencies can actually be used as real money.

Chapter Two:

Understanding Blockchain Technology

If you have heard a thing or two about cryptocurrencies, you may have heard about the blockchain, which is the technology that powers Bitcoin and hundreds of other cryptocurrencies. Beyond this common definition, do you know what the blockchain really is? Do you know how it works?

The blockchain as we know it today is the ingenious brainchild of Bitcoin's pseudonymous inventor, Satoshi Nakamoto. Described simply, the blockchain is a decentralized public and permanent record of transactions. In other words, the blockchain is a public ledger where entries cannot be altered once they have been added. However, it is also decentralized. What does this mean?

Decentralization means that there is no central authority in charge of the power to make decisions. Instead, this responsibility is delegated to all organization members. With the blockchain, this responsibility rests with all the computers within the network. Therefore, no one entity can regulate the blockchain. Instead, the members relate with each other based on mathematical rules that all of them have to obey. If a decision or transaction has to be made, all the computers in the network have to agree that it has indeed occurred in order for it to be verified. To make the concept of decentralization easier to understand, I will use an illustration.

Traditionally, when two people wanted to collaborate on a document, one person would work on the document and send it to the other person so that they could add their revisions to it. In this scenario, the first person cannot see the changes made by the other person until a copy of the revised document is sent back. The first person would also need to wait for the revised document to be sent back before making any further changes. In the end, it would be up to one person to decide which version should be used as the correct version. However, if the two people were to use the software Google Docs, both of them would simultaneously have access to the document. Both could make changes at the same time and the latest version of the document would be available to both of them at the same time.

Having to send the document for changes to be made can be compared to how databases work today. This is the system used by banks to process money balances and transfers. Access is briefly locked on one side, the transfer is made and then access is reopened. The blockchain, on the other hand, can be compared to the Google Doc application, where everyone has the same record of the public ledger at all times. However, instead of being shared between two people, the blockchain is distributed among several people. However, the blockchain takes it a step further. Instead of having one person make a decision on which document should be used as the correct version, all the people with access to the document have to come to an agreement on the correct version. Doing this gives the blockchain a robustness that is similar to that of the internet. It cannot be controlled by any one person and it has no single point of failure.

Just like the Google Doc app, the blockchain is always in a state of consensus. It checks in with itself every few minutes and automatically updates itself to the latest version on all nodes. The groups of transactions between each automatic update is known as a block. The constant state of consensus has two effects. First, it enhances transparency since the latest version of the database is visible by everyone within the network. More importantly, it means that the blockchain cannot be corrupted. Corrupting the blockchain would mean gaining control of a majority of the computers in the network. While this seems possible in theory, it is very unlikely to happen since it would need massive amounts of computational power. Taking control of the blockchain would also destroy the value of the cryptocurrencies.

A Network of Nodes

The blockchain is made up of a network of computers known as nodes. These computers run the blockchain protocol, allowing them to send and receive messages from each other. Nodes can join the network voluntarily. Once a new node joins the network, it automatically downloads the latest version of the blockchain. These nodes are one of the most important elements of any blockchain network. Once a node joins the network, it becomes a co-administrator on the network. It is given the responsibility of helping to verify every single transaction that is made on the blockchain. After verification, the node records the transaction to a block. This goes on until a block is complete, after which the node adds it to the blockchain. The chance of winning newly created coins acts as an incentive for the nodes to perform these administrative tasks on the blockchain network.

When a user sends coins to another user, the nodes check the transaction data to ensure the validity of the transaction. It compares the transaction data with its version of the blockchain and ascertains that the coins have not been double spent. In the event that the node determines that the transaction data is invalid, it automatically rejects the transaction. It also rejects any further communication with the node that sent the transaction. Nodes have a non-trust based relationship with other nodes on the network. Therefore, if one node sends invalid data to the other nodes, they immediately cut communication with this node and ban it from the network.

However, if the node ascertains that the transaction data is valid, the transaction is forwarded to miners. Miners group transactions together based on chronological order to form blocks. Once a block is completed, it is passed back to the nodes for verification. All validation is done by nodes since it is impossible for them to propagate incorrect information. Once the nodes confirm the validity of a block, they can now add it to the blockchain.

The effectiveness of blockchain technology is based on the following three principle technologies:

Private Key Cryptography

The blockchain makes it possible for people to make transactions over the internet without the need for a trusted third party. However, for the transaction to be safe and secure, there has to be a form of trust. On the internet, trust boils down to two things – authentication (proof of identity) and authorization (proof of permissions). Put simply, there has to be a way of verifying that someone is indeed who they say they are and that they have the permission to do whatever they are trying to do.

In the case of blockchain technology, trust is established through the use of private key cryptography. Cryptography relies on mathematics to encrypt information into secret code that cannot be accessed by unauthorized entities. For one to access the information, they need a key to decrypt the information.

A cryptocurrency transaction basically involves someone sending encrypted data to another person. Whenever someone makes a transaction on the blockchain, the transaction is encrypted using cryptographic keys. For every transaction, two mathematically linked keys – a public and a private key – are generated. For one to make an encrypted transaction, the public key is needed. To decrypt the transaction, one has to have the private key. The private key is the cryptocurrency wallet address, which allows anyone to send encrypted data (the crypto coins) to the owner of the wallet. However, for the owner receive the coins, they have to decrypt the data using their private key. The private key shows that you are the owner of the wallet address. The private key also confirms that you have permission to transact, i.e. you have enough coins to make transactions. Through the private key, the blockchain confirms authenticity and authorization, thereby solving the issue of trust.

A Distributed Network

For the blockchain to be effective, authentication and authorization are not enough. There is also need for a distributed peer-to-peer network. This network helps solve the issue of security and record-keeping. For transactions to be accepted as valid, they have to be confirmed by the entire network. This can be explained using a famous thought experiment known as the 'if a tree falls in the forest'. However, our thought experiment will be tweaked slightly.

If a tree fell in a forest and there are two cameras recording the event, then we can be certain that the tree actually fell since there is visual evidence of the event. However, if one camera recorded the falling of the tree while the other did not, then we cannot be certain that the tree actually fell. This is the concept behind the value of the blockchain network. The nodes within the network are the cameras in our analogy. If the nodes are in consensus that the event happened at a particular time, then there is certainty that the event happened. For a transaction to be confirmed as valid, the majority of the nodes have to reach consensus that the transaction actually happened. However, instead of using cameras, the nodes use mathematical puzzles for validation.

When private key cryptography is combined with this distributed network, the blockchain becomes more effective. A person, using their private key to prove authenticity and authorization, announces to the network that they are making a transaction, the whole network watches the transaction and confirms that it has indeed occurred.

An Incentive for Security and Record-Keeping

While the combination of private key cryptography and a distributed network seems foolproof, it has one flaw. Why should the nodes be waiting to observe and confirm that a transaction has indeed taken place? Put differently, how does the network attract nodes to confirm transactions and thus make the network secure? This is where mining comes in. By performing administrative tasks and ensuring the security of the network, the nodes are rewarded with newly created coins. The self-interest of the nodes is used for public good.

Chapter Three:

Different Types of Cryptocurrency

Mention the word cryptocurrency and most people will instantly think about Bitcoin. For some, cryptocurrency is an alternative name for Bitcoin. This is because Bitcoin was the trendsetter, the leader amongst a growing wave of cryptocurrencies based on a decentralized P2P network. However, there is more to cryptocurrencies than just Bitcoin. So far, there are over 1500 different types of cryptocurrencies. Many more are being introduced into the world every single day. With Bitcoin having identified itself as the leader in the world of cryptographic currencies, the other cryptocurrencies are known as 'altcoins', which simply means that they are alternatives to Bitcoin. Most of these altcoins were inspired by Bitcoin. Many use a variation of the Bitcoin protocol, with some changes made to reflect their core objective. However, not all altcoins are variants of Bitcoin. Some developers have built their altcoins from scratch, with their own distinctive core framework.

Despite the existence of thousands of cryptocurrencies, only a handful have any relevance. Of these, even less have managed to achieve a market capitalization of over $1 million. In this chapter, we will take a look at some of the most relevant cryptocurrencies.

Bitcoin (BTC)

This is the world's first and most known modern-day cryptocurrency. Even though most people might not understand much about it, almost everyone has heard about Bitcoin. Bitcoin is a peer-to-peer (p2p) digital payment system that facilitates *instant* transactions without having to go through an intermediary. Bitcoin was first introduced into the world in October 2008, when someone using the pseudonym Satoshi Nakamoto published a white paper outlining the architecture and working method of the cryptocurrency. In January 2009, Nakamoto mined the first Bitcoin Block (referred to as the Genesis block), thereby creating the first Bitcoins. By developing Bitcoin, Nakamoto's objective was to transfer the control of money from banks and governments to the people, in the same way that the internet transferred control over information to the people.

New Bitcoins are created as a reward for mining, which is what keeps the Bitcoin protocol running. The Bitcoin protocol is configured in a way that keeps the rate of production of new Bitcoins around a certain average. If more processing power is deployed to mine for new Bitcoins, mining becomes harder. If some processing power is taken from the network, the difficulty of mining for new Bitcoins decreases. The protocol was created with a limit of 21 million Bitcoins, after which no more Bitcoins will be released.

Bitcoin was developed to be a payment system, therefore people can use Bitcoin to buy goods and services both on the internet and offline. Currently, there are hundreds of thousands of businesses that accept Bitcoin payments. Apart from using Bitcoin to pay for goods and services, Bitcoin can also be traded against other currencies or held as an investment. Holding Bitcoin as an investment asset has become particularly popular in 2017, which saw the price of one Bitcoin rise from below $1000 at the beginning of the year to almost $20,000 towards the end of the year.

Bitcoin can be divided into smaller units known as millibitcoins, microbitcoins and satoshi's. The smallest unit of Bitcoin is the Satoshi (0.00000001), which was named in honor of Bitcoin's mysterious inventor. As the first ever modern cryptocurrency, Bitcoin is the easiest to get and enjoys the widest acceptance. Bitcoin is also the largest, with a market capitalization of over $300 billion, which exceeds the combined market cap of the altcoins in this list.

Ethereum (ETH)

Ethereum comes second to Bitcoin in terms of popularity and market capitalization. Just like Bitcoin, Ethereum is an open source, decentralized platform that is based on blockchain technology. Unlike Bitcoin, however, Ethereum is not a payment platform. Instead, it is a platform that allows developers to build and deploy various kinds of blockchain based decentralized applications, which are referred to as DApps. The tokens or coins of the Ethereum protocol are known as Ether. One of the most outstanding features of Ethereum is 'smart contracts', which are lines of code that allow the transfer of value with zero risk of fraud or interference. This means that apart from money, smart contracts can be used on the Ethereum platform to transfer other valuables such as shares, land titles and car ownership, to mention a few. Ethereum was created and launched in 2015 by Vitalik Buterin, a young Russian-Canadian programmer.

In the long run, Ethereum holds much more promise than Bitcoin. While the two competing cryptocurrencies both rely on blockchain technology, they have major differences in terms of objective and capability. Bitcoin is strictly a payment system, which is only one application of blockchain technology. Instead of focusing on one use like Bitcoin did, Ethereum allows developers to build all kinds of decentralized apps. This means that Ethereum has the capability of revolutionizing all services and sectors that are currently centralized. Just like Bitcoin, the value of Ethereum has grown exponentially in 2017. The price of one Ether has soared from below $10 at the beginning of the year to over $750 towards the end of the year. Today, Ethereum has a market capitalization of about $83 billion.

Today, there are two parallel Ethereum blockchains, Ethereum (ETH) and Ethereum Classic (ETC). Ethereum Classic was introduced after a split that came following the hacking of the Ethereum based DAO project in September of 2016, where about $50 million worth of Ether was stolen.

Litecoin (LTC)

Litecoin is among one of the first cryptocurrencies to be launched following the emergence of Bitcoin. Unsatisfied with the long wait times of Bitcoin transactions, a Google software engineer named Charles Lee decided to create his own alternative to Bitcoin, which he launched in 2011 and named Litecoin. By launching Litecoin, Lee's objective was to make small but effective changes which would improve the efficiency of Bitcoin and other cryptocurrencies that relied on the proof of work (POW) verification system.

One of the major changes that Lee made was the cryptographic hash function used by Litecoin. Unlike Bitcoin which uses the SHA256 hash, Lee introduced 'scrypt' in Litecoin. Switching to 'scrypt' allowed Litecoin to process and confirm transactions faster. Litecoin transactions are verified in about two minutes, while Bitcoin might take up to 10 minutes to verify transactions. Another advantage of using 'scrypt' is that it allowed users with consumer grade CPUs to mine for coins, unlike Bitcoin which requires miners to have CPUs that are specialized for mining.

Lee maintained the built-in scarcity that is characteristic of Bitcoin. However, Litecoin has a limit of 84 million coins as opposed to Bitcoin's 21 million. By doing so, Lee gave Litecoin more liquidity, since there are more coins available for purchase, preventing the hoarding that has become so common with Bitcoin buyers. Another major difference between Litecoin and Bitcoin is that Litecoin uses a slightly different mining protocol, which allows fairer distribution of mined coins. Litecoin also allows for faster testing and implementation of new technology. For instance, Litecoin pioneered and implemented SegWit (Segregated Witness) technology way before Bitcoin. All in all, Litecoin is a strong cryptocurrency with a good reputation and solid economic principles. Litecoin currently has a market capitalization of about $19 billion.

IOTA (IOT)

The developers of IOTA built it with the objective of making it the backbone for the Internet of Things (IOT). The Internet of Things refers to the network of internet-enabled day to day physical objects which use embedded sensors to collect and transmit data. IOT includes things like internet enabled cars, computers, kitchen appliances, microchips, home automation devices, hospital devices, and so on. By being the backbone of IOT, IOTA aims to achieve its call of being the 'Ledger of Everything'.

Apart from simply being the backbone of IOT, IOTA was also developed to solve some of the challenges faced by Bitcoin, including issues of scalability, speed and transaction fees. IOTA has one key difference between it and other cryptocurrencies like Bitcoin. Whereas Bitcoin and most other cryptocurrencies are based on blockchain technology, IOTA is based on something known as the 'Tangle'. The Tangle is a Directed Acyclic Graph (DAG), a different kind of distributed ledger whose protocol is different from the blockchain protocol.

With blockchain based cryptocurrencies, the network of computers need to verify a transaction before it is completed. With the Tangle, verification does not rely on the network. Instead, the Tangle relies on a system that requires the sender to perform some proof of work before they can make their transaction. By doing so, the sender approves two transactions, thereby combining the transaction and its verification. Since it is up to the sender to provide the proof of work, there is no need for miners.

This has two benefits. First, by eliminating miners, the Tangle makes IOTA fully decentralized. Instead of having players who have an effect on the network without actually using it (miners simply enable the network, but they are not using it), the IOTA network is maintained solely by the 'users' who are actually making transactions. Second, by having the sender approve two transactions before they can make their transaction, this system makes the IOTA protocol faster. It also means that an increase in the number of users leads to a faster validation speed. This is unlike what normally happens with other cryptocurrencies like Bitcoin, where an increase in the number of users slows down the validation time. Since there are no miners, users do not have to pay any fees for maintaining the network either. IOTA has seen a positive growth in 2017, with its market capitalization rising to $11 billion by the end of 2017.

Ripple (XRP)

Ripple is a platform that was designed to enable real-time global settlements as well as to act as a currency exchange and remittance network. The Ripple tokens are not meant to be used as a means of paying for goods and services. Instead, the network was designed with the objective of allowing instant conversions between different fiat currencies without having to rely on a central exchange. Since its release in 2012, a number of banks have adopted Ripple as a cost effective way of processing international payments.

Unlike many cryptocurrencies out there, Ripple was not built as a variant of Bitcoin. Instead, its developers built it from scratch and incorporated some major changes in its architecture. Unlike most cryptocurrencies which use a proof of stake or proof of work system to verify transactions, Ripple uses a unique consensus system where the computers in the network keep monitoring any changes. Once majority of the computers in the network observe a transaction, it is added to the public ledger. The consensus system has a number of advantages over the proof of work or proof of stake systems. Transactions verified under the consensus system are validated faster and require less processing power. While it might seem possible for hackers to compromise the consensus system, it is designed in such a way that any unreliable results are rejected by the network.

Since the Ripple network is meant to facilitate cross-currency conversions, Ripples can be exchanged for a wide range of fiat currencies and altcoins. Some businesses also allow customers to exchange Ripples for air miles and reward points. Unlike altcoins like Ether and Litecoin which are sold on cryptocurrency exchanges, you have to go through Gateways to buy Ripples. The Gateways work in the same way PayPal works. Ripple currently has a market capitalization of about $30 billion.

Dash (Dash)

Dash is a cryptocurrency that was developed by Evan Duffield and Kyle Hagan. Launched in 2014, it was originally known as Darkcoin. After a year in existence, it rebranded to Dash, which is the shortened version of Digital Cash. By developing Dash, Kyle and Evan wanted to create a cryptocurrency that is totally secret and anonymous. Most cryptocurrencies are not totally anonymous. Though addresses are not linked to personally identifiable information, the network knows the number of coins within each address and anyone can keep track of coins as they move from one address to another. This makes it possible for someone to know the identity of users who do not take measures to protect their identity. To keep users anonymous, Dash uses a decentralized mastercode network which makes Dash transactions practically impossible to trace.

The high level of anonymity offered by Dash is enabled by a system known as Darksend. With this system, specialized computers known as mastercodes collect several transactions and execute them simultaneously, thereby keeping the transaction untraceable. It becomes impossible to track the source and destination of the coins. To make your transactions even more anonymous, you can choose to have the mastercodes mix your transaction for multiple rounds before completing the transaction. To maintain this anonymity, the Dash ledger is not publicly accessible. The high level of anonymity has also prevented wide acceptance by businesses.

Another distinguishing feature of Dash is its hashing algorithm. Instead of using the SHA256 or scrypt hash, Dash uses a unique X11 hash which requires less processing power, allowing users with consumer grade CPUs to mine for Dash coins. Other notable advantages of Dash include its fast transaction verification of about 4 seconds and low transaction fees. However, the fees are likely to rise once more people join the network. Dash also has a voting system in place to allow the quick implementation of important changes. Capped at around $9 billion, Dash also has an exceptionally high price per coin for altcoins.

Monero (XMR)

Monero is another cryptocurrency that, just like Dash, is focused on privacy and anonymity. Monero was launched in 2014 by a team of 7 programmers, 5 of whom chose to remain anonymous. Due to its anonymity features, it quickly gained popularity with cryptocurrency enthusiasts. Like most other cryptocurrencies, Monero is totally open source. Development of the platform is driven by the community and donations. Monero is based on a particularly strong cryptography protocol known as 'CryptoNote'. It also uses a unique hash known as 'CryptoNight'. To ensure complete anonymity and privacy, Monero uses the 'ring signatures' technique. This technique is a digital version of group signatures. Each transaction on the Monero network is enshrouded by a group of cryptographic signatures. This way, it is impossible to pinpoint the actual sender or recipient in the transaction. Even with a person's wallet address, it is impossible to see the amount of coins in the wallet or keep track of where they are spent. This means that it is impossible for Monero coins to become tainted as a result of previous dubious transactions.

Monero transactions are verified using the same proof of work system that Bitcoin uses. However, a major difference between Bitcoin and Monero is that whereas Bitcoin block sizes are limited at 2MB, there is no limitation on Monero block sizes. The lack of limited block sizes presents the risk of malicious miners using disproportionately huge blocks to clog up the system. To ensure this does not happen, the system has an inbuilt block reward penalty system. This means that whenever a miner mines a new block that exceeds the median size of the last 100 blocks, their block reward is reduced depending on how much the new block exceeds the median size of the last 100 blocks. The current market cap of Monero is $5 billion.

Neo (NEO)

Neo is a Chinese cryptocurrency that was founded by Erik Zhang and Da Hongfei. Neo is designed to be a smart economy platform, much like Ethereum. It has even been referred to as 'China's Ethereum'. Neo was first launched under the name Antshares. In August 2017, it rebranded to NEO Smart Contract Economy. NEO's objective is very similar to that of Ethereum. NEO provides a platform where developers can develop decentralized applications and deploy smart contracts. Unlike Ethereum, which only supports its Solidity programming language, NEO can be used with common programming languages such as C#, Python and Java.

One of the key differences between NEO and Ethereum lies in the verification system used by each of them. Whereas Ethereum uses a combination of proof of stake or proof of work verification, NEO relies on a consensus system referred to as a Delegated Byzantine Fault Tolerance (dBFT). In this system, instead of having all the computers in the system participate in verification, certain nodes are designated as bookkeepers. It is up to these bookkeepers to verify blocks before they are added to the blockchain. If two-thirds or more of the computers on the network are in agreement with the bookkeeper's version, consensus is achieved and the new block is validated and written to the blockchain. If consensus cannot be achieved, another bookkeeper is called up and the whole process is repeated.

Since consensus under the dBFT system only needs to be achieved by a subset of the network, this system requires less processing power and allows the network to handle a higher transaction volume. NEO claims that it is capable of handling over 1000 transactions per second, whereas Ethereum only handles 15 transactions per second. The dBFT system also eliminates the possibility of a hard fork, which makes NEO a great option for digitizing real-world financial assets. The current market capitalization of NEO is about $4 billion.

OmiseGO (OMG)

OmiseGO is a cryptocurrency that has gained a lot of popularity from cryptocurrency enthusiasts lately. Launched in 2013, it is an interesting yet very ambitious project whose aim is to use Ethereum based financial technology to un-bank the banked. OmiseGO is currently built on the Ethereum platform as an ERC20 token, though it will eventually launch its own blockchain. OmiseGO's vision is to become the leading p2p cryptocurrency exchange platform. Instead of being just an altcoins, OmiseGO is built to act as a financial platform with the aim of disrupting the financial sector as we currently know it.

OmiseGO aims to solve a challenge that most cryptocurrency exchanges have failed to address. To purchase a cryptocurrency in most cryptocurrency exchanges, you have to start with a fiat currency. To exchange one altcoin for another, you have to convert the altcoins to fiat or Bitcoin and then convert the fiat/Bitcoin back to your desired altcoins. Throughout this process, the exchange charges fees for each transaction. This means that you will pay fees to convert the first altcoins to fiat/Bitcoin and pay the fees again to convert the fiat/Bitcoin to the second altcoins.

OmiseGO plans to solve this problem by linking all existing cryptocurrency wallets to a central OmiseGO blockchain. This way, users can easily exchange altcoins for other altcoins without having to convert them to fiat or Bitcoin. This means that instead of multiple fees, users will only pay one tiny fee.

OmiseGO also aims to bring decentralization to cryptocurrency exchanges. Currently, most exchanges are centralized operations. The records of all transactions as well as data about different users is stored in databases which are stored on the company's servers. OmiseGO aims to decentralize the exchange functionality by having all the transactions info and user data stored on the blockchain. This way, the data is more secure since a hacker would then need to perform a 51% attack (gaining control over 51% of the computers in the network) in order to breach the blockchain, which is virtually impossible. OmiseGO currently has a market capitalization of about $1 billion.

NEM (XEM)

NEM is a revolutionary cryptocurrency that was launched in March 2015. Unlike many other cryptocurrencies which were created as variants of existing projects, NEM was built from the ground up, with its own unique source code. NEM derived its name from the New Economic Movement, the group which came up with the cryptocurrency. NEM is designed as a blockchain based technology that can be customized to fit different business purposes. At the core of NEM's protocol is what is known as the 'Smart Asset System'.

Since NEM can be customized to fit multiple use cases, it has unlimited potential uses. It can be used as a central ledger in the banking sector, a means of keeping secure records, a blockchain-based voting system, an escrow service, as a means of rewarding points in loyalty programs, crowd funding, stock ownership and so on. This shows how much potential NEM holds.

Unlike most cryptocurrency platforms, NEM has a messaging platform. It also has a reward system and supports multisig transactions. One of the key differences between NEM and other cryptocurrencies is the verification method. Instead of proof of work or proof of stake, NEM relies on a unique proof of importance system where block calculation chances are allocated based on the contribution of a user to the development and distribution of the platform. Users who make a lot of contribution get rewarded with more chances. This allows fair distribution of mining chances among users.

The NEM network is fast, with a transaction verification wait time of about one minute. This means that you can rely on NEM to make instant global money transfers. With the proof of importance system, users don't need expensive hardware to mine NEM coins. The market capitalization of NEM currently stands at about $8 billion.

Chapter Four:

How to Hold Your Coins Safely and Securely

The last one year has seen tremendous growth of interest in cryptocurrencies by investors, the banking industry, the media and the general public. This interest has led to a merciless bullish run in the cryptocurrency market, with all popular cryptocurrencies seeing a significant increase in value. In 2017, the value of one Bitcoin rose from below $1000 in January to almost $20000 towards the end of the year, while the value of Ethereum rose from below $10 to over $750 in the same period. With most other popular cryptocurrencies seeing similar surges in value, it comes as no surprise that cryptocurrency is attracting unsolicited interest from hackers. In this chapter, we will look at how you can keep your cryptocurrency wallet safe from prying hackers.

What is a Cryptocurrency Wallet?

In real life, you normally keep your paper money in a wallet. Similarly, before you buy a cryptocurrency, you need to have a wallet to keep your coins. Unlike a normal wallet, a cryptocurrency wallet is not a physical object. It is a basically a software program that allows you to receive, send and monitor the balance of your crypto coins. The wallet consists of two 'keys', a public key and a private key. The public key is your wallet address. This is what other people use to send you coins. The private key is what allows you to send your coins to others. To send your coins, you are actually signing off ownership of the coins using your private key.

To make it easier to understand the concept of public and private keys, I will use an illustration. Your public address is like a vending machine. Anyone can put money into a vending machine. Similarly, anyone with your wallet's public key can send you money. However, to get money from the vending machine, the owner needs an actual key to the machine. Without the key, no one can remove the money from the machine. This is represented by your private key. To access and use the money in your cryptocurrency wallet, you need the private key. Anyone with your private key can access and spend your coins. Hackers steal your coins by stealing your private key. It's important to note that the cryptocurrency wallet does not actually store your coins, it only stores the keys that you need to send and receive the coins. When you send or receive coins, no coins are actually exchanged. Instead, the transaction is simply a record on the blockchain that changes the balance in your cryptocurrency wallet.

Choosing A Cryptocurrency Wallet

Today, there is a wide variety of cryptocurrency wallets to choose from, which makes choosing the right one a challenge, especially if you are just getting started with cryptocurrency. Making the right choice boils down to striking a balance between the security of your coins and convenience. To make the choice easier, you need to consider the following two variables: transaction value and transaction volume. Transaction value is the amount of coins you need to transact at a time, while the transaction volume refers to how frequently you will need to send or receive coins in a given period of time. There is no absolute figure for these two variables. They are relative and will vary for different people.

Let's take a look at the different types of wallets and how the above variables influence which wallet you should use.

Online Wallets

Also known as cloud wallets, these are the simplest to use and are also very convenient. Online wallets store their keys online. If you intend to have low transaction volume and value, an online wallet is an excellent choice. This means that you should opt for an online wallet if you intend to store fairly small amounts of coins and make relatively few transactions. While the term 'low transaction value' is relative, you should only store your coins on an online wallet if you would be comfortable walking around with a similar amount of money in your pockets on the street. Access to an online wallet only requires an email address and password, which makes them quite easy to use. Since they can be accessed from any location with an internet connection, they are also very convenient. However, since they store their keys on the internet, online wallets are the most vulnerable to hacking attacks. You should ensure your online wallet has a very strong password to keep your coins secure.

Mobile Wallets

Mobile wallets are also very user-friendly and are the most convenient to use. These are a good choice for someone who intends to frequently send or receive low amounts of cryptocurrency. For example, someone who frequently makes cryptocurrency payments to gain access to online gaming platforms should consider using a mobile wallet. The convenience of mobile wallets stems from the fact that most people always carry their smart phones with them. This allows them to make on-the-spot cryptocurrency payments. Mobile wallets offer better security in comparison to online wallets. To avoid losing access to your coins in case you lose your phone, you should note down your seed phrase on a piece of paper and keep it safely.

Paper Wallets

Paper wallets have a fairly good amount of security. However, they are the least convenient to use. As such, you should only consider a paper wallet if you intend to store huge amounts of cryptocurrency while making relatively few transactions. To ensure maximum security for your coins, you should set up your paper wallet yourself instead of relying on an online service. One thing you should note about paper wallets is that you cannot spend your coins directly from the paper wallet. To spend the coins, you need to import your private key into another wallet. If you are not careful during this process, you might negate all the precautions you took while setting up the paper wallet.

Hardware Wallets

Hardware wallets offer the highest level of security. They are also quite convenient. This makes them a great choice if you intend to make high value transactions every now and then. Most hardware wallets look like USB flash drives. However, unlike flash drives, they do not have any storage space for your media and other files. Instead, they are fitted with a specialized chip that stores your wallet's private key. This allows them to keep your coins safe even in the event that a malicious person gains access to your computer. Hardware wallets require a password for access to the wallet's private key, which keeps your coins secure even in the event that someone manages to steal your hardware wallet. As is the case with mobile wallets, you should jot down your seed phrase on a piece of paper and keep it safely. This allows you to retrieve your coins if your hardware wallet gets lost or damaged. Unlike the other kinds of wallets which are free, you have to pay for a hardware wallet.

Desired Traits of a Cryptocurrency Wallet

Apart from considering the transaction value and transaction volume when choosing the type of wallet you require, there are other factors that you should keep in mind when it comes to choosing the actual wallet. These are:

Cost: Some wallets are free while you have to pay for others. Are you willing to spend money to keep your coins safe?

Security: Does the company that provides the wallet have a good record of excellent security? Have there ever been any security breaches within the company?

Mobility: Can you access you wallet any place, any time?

User-friendliness: Does the wallet have an intuitive design? Does it support different kinds of cryptocurrency?

Convenience: Can you easily make a fast transaction when you need to?

Style: This is mostly for people who are looking for cool tech gadgets.

Ideally, a great cryptocurrency wallet should have a combination of the above traits, based on your personal needs and preferences. Below are some popular wallets that you can consider:

Bread Wallet: This is a simple mobile wallet that can be downloaded from the App Store. Bread Wallet makes the process of sending Bitcoins as simple as sending an email. This wallet is a standalone client, which means that it stores your keys on your phone and not on any server. Bread Wallet offers good privacy and security, has a clean, intuitive and lightweight design and is free to use. However, Bread Wallet only supports Bitcoin.

Mycelium: This is a strong and secure Bitcoin mobile wallet that is better suited for advanced users. The wallet is available for both Android and iOs devices and gives users total control over their Bitcoins. Mycelium comes with enterprise level security and offers advanced features like encrypted PDF backups, cold storage, secure chat, a local trading marketplace, an integrated QR code scanner and many more. This is one of the best free Bitcoin mobile wallets available.

Exodus: This is relatively new digital wallet that currently works on PCs only. Exodus has an intuitive and beautiful interface that is very easy to use. Exodus allows you to store and trade Bitcoins, Litecoins, Dash, Ether, Dogecoins and several other altcoins. One of Exodus's key features is that it has an integrated Shapeshift exchange which allows you to trade altcoins within the app. Exodus is free to use.

Copay: This is a great free digital wallet that is available online, on mobile and on PC. Copay has a user friendly interface that is beginner friendly, though it also has a set of geeky features that will impress advanced users as well. One of the greatest features of Copay is that it supports multisig transactions.

Jaxx: This is another popular wallet that supports multiple cryptocurrencies, including Bitcoin, Ether, Ether Classic, Zcash, REP, Rootstock, DAO, Dash and Litecoin. Jaxx supports a number of platforms, including Windows, OSX, Linux, Android and iOS. It is also available online through Chrome and Firefox extensions. Just like Exodus, it also has an integrated Shapeshift exchange.

Armory: This is an open source desktop wallet that is solely focused on security. It has an awesome set of security features that advanced users will love, including cold storage, one-time printable backups, support for multisig transactions, GPU-resistant wallet transactions, multiple wallets interface, Key importing and sweeping and many more. However, this wallet is not very suitable for beginners. Armory supports Bitcoin only.

Trezor: This is one of the best hardware Bitcoin wallets. Trezor is built to be malware-resistant. It comes with an intuitive interface that is supported on Windows, Linux and OSX. Trezor offers great security, but you have to part with $99 for the wallet.

Ledger Nano: This is another multisig hardware wallet that uses a second layer of security to eliminate various attack vectors. Ledger Nano supports multiple cryptocurrencies and allows users to run 3rd party apps from the device. It also comes with a screen that allows you to perform some operations without connecting the device to a computer. The Ledger Nano costs about $65.

Green Address: This is a simplistic, user-friendly Bitcoin wallet that is an excellent choice for those who are just getting started with cryptocurrency. Green Address has desktop and mobile apps and is also available online. This wallet has many security features, including multisig addresses, paper wallet backups, 2-Factor authentication and instant transaction confirmation. However, you do not have total control over your coins since payments have to be approved by Green Address.

Blockchain.info: This is a very popular online Bitcoin wallet. For better security, Blockchain.info uses 2-factor authentication for browsers while the mobile application requests a password every time it is opened. While your wallet is stored online, Blockchain.info is not privy to your private keys. Overall, this is a good online wallet that has earned trust in the Bitcoin community.

Other Important Things to Keep in Mind When Securing Your Coins

Never Leave Your Coins On Exchanges

This is one rule every cryptocurrency user should abide by. Once your buy your crypto coins, immediately transfer them to your wallet. By leaving them on the exchange, you put yourself at risk of losing your coins in case the exchange shuts down or gets hacked (as happened with MtGox and Cryptsy).

Keep Your Assets in A Wallet Where You Have Control Over the Keys

Whoever is in control of the keys to your wallet has control over your funds. Therefore, you should only store your coins in a wallet that gives you total control over your keys. When you leave your coins on the exchange or store them in online wallets that have access to your keys, you are basically handing over the responsibility of keeping your coins safe to these third parties. You should also consider using a unique passphrase to encrypt your wallet for extra security.

Use 2-Factor Authentication On Exchanges

Always secure your exchange accounts with 2-factor authentication. Sometimes, it is necessary to transfer your assets to exchanges when you need to trade. In such instances, a hacker who has compromised your password can easily steal your crypto coins. However, with 2-factor authentication, they would need also need your 2FA code before logging into your account. Since these codes are usually sent to your phone via text message, it would be impossible for an attacker to log into your account unless they had access to your phone.

Take Care When Sending Coins to Others

When sending coins to another user, it is quite easy to erroneously send them to the wrong address. Since cryptocurrency transactions are irreversible, this means that your coins will be gone for good. To avoid such occurrences, you should first send a small amount of cryptocurrency to the address you intend to send to. If that transaction goes on correctly, you can then move large amounts of cryptocurrency with the assurance that you are sending them to the correct address.

Always Backup Your Wallets

Always keep several online and offline backups of your cryptocurrency wallets. For instance, Exodus offers online backups that allow you to restore your wallet via email. You can also use a USB flash drive or write down your private keys on a piece of paper and keep them in a safe place.

With everything you have learnt in this chapter, you should be able to keep your coins safe from loss and theft by malicious hackers. You should also always remember the golden rule of cryptocurrency: Whoever controls the keys controls the assets.

Chapter Five:

Cryptocurrency Mining

The term cryptocurrency mining is derived from the fact that new coins are created (mined) whenever new transactions are recorded on the blockchain. Mining is an essential aspect of how most cryptocurrencies work. In order for a user to send or receive crypto coins, the user initiates a transaction which is then broadcast to the entire network. Before this transaction can be completed, it has to be validated and recorded on the public ledger.

This process is what is referred to as mining. The cryptocurrency networks rely on miners to validate transactions and add them to the public ledger and to ensure that users are not trying to trick the system. New crypto coins are also created and added to the network through the process of mining. As a reward for mining, miners are issued these newly created coins. In other words, miners act as bookkeepers for the cryptocurrency network and earn small fees and newly created coins as payment. Anyone can become a cryptocurrency miner as long as they have internet access and sufficient computer hardware.

The Block Reward

Cryptocurrency mining is based around the concept of block rewards. For cryptocurrency transactions to be verified, miners are required to solve complex, computationally demanding mathematical equations. The solutions to these mathematical puzzles are based on the results of the previous block solutions, therefore it is impossible for a miner to calculate the solution of a future block in advance without the solution to the previous block. A block is simply a collection of the cryptographic signatures of the transactions made within a specific period of time. The blockchain is formed by this history of block transactions and solutions.

The computers mining the cryptocurrency are essentially competing with one another to solve these puzzles. The first computer to come up with a solution for the puzzles gets to add the next block to the blockchain. In return, this computer is rewarded with newly created coins and the fees charged for the transactions. This is what is known as the block reward.

Most cryptocurrencies are designed with a maximum number of coins that can be possibly released within the network. For instance, the maximum number of Bitcoins that will be produced is 21 million coins, while Litecoin has a limit of 84 million coins. To ensure that all the coins do not get mined at once, different cryptocurrencies employ different methods of controlling the rate at which new coins are released.

For most cryptocurrencies, the computational demanding mathematical puzzles have a difficulty value that can scale up or down over time depending on the effort miners are using to mine the cryptocurrency. The aim of this is to keep the rate of release of new coins fairly constant. For instance, the difficulty level of Bitcoins mathematical puzzles is set to adjust itself after every 2016 blocks mined, or once about every two weeks. When the computational power put into mining is increased, the difficulty level increases. When the computation power is decreased, the puzzles become easier to solve. By doing so,

Bitcoin targets to have a block solution generated about every 10 minutes. Different cryptocurrencies have different approaches. For instance, the target for Ethereum is a block solution after every 16 seconds.

Cryptocurrency mining and the block reward can be compared to panning for gold in a stream. Some will get lucky and find huge gold nuggets, others will only find some gold dust while others will not find anything. Whoever is in a good location will find more gold. However, with cryptocurrency, the good location is represented by good mining hardware.

Setting Up Mining Software

There are several options when it comes to cryptocurrency mining. Some algorithms like CryptoNight can be run on CPUs. Others like Ethereum, Vertcoin and Zcash are best run on GPUs, while others like Bitcoin and Litecoin can only be run on ASICs (Application Specific Integrated Circuits). However, there's more to mining besides having the mining hardware.

During the early days of cryptocurrency, it was possible for someone to solo-mine. All you had to do was to download or build a wallet for your preferred cryptocurrency and install the correct mining software. You would then configure the mining software to join your preferred cryptocurrency network and task your hardware with running the calculations in the hope of finding a valid block solution before other miners.

These days, however, a lot of things have changed. You don't need to have the wallet software, since it is no longer necessary for mining and only ends up eating up your disk space and bandwidth. For instance, downloading the Bitcoin blockchain will take up about 145GB. Nowadays, websites have been built up to take care of this. However, this also led to the increase in the number of people who are mining cryptocurrencies. Ideally, if you provide a certain percentage of the total computational power expended in mining a particular cryptocurrency, you should find an equal percentage of all the blocks mined. However, with the increase in the number of miners, it is impossible to provide any substantial amount of computational power, which in turn means that your chances of finding a valid block solution is virtually impossible. This is where mining pools come in.

Mining Pools

With the increasing number of miners, solo mining is virtually impossible. To win block rewards, you have to become part of large mining guilds, which are referred to as mining pools. When it comes to mining, the bigger the mining pool, the higher the chances of finding valid block solutions. However, it is important to note that for security purposes, no single individual or mining group is allowed to have control of more than 50 percent of the total computational power (hashrate) in any cryptocurrency network. This would lead to what is known as a 51% attack.

Mining pools work by having every participant contribute their computational power to mining. Similarly, all rewards are distributed among all the pool members based on the percentage of computational power they provide. Your hardware is assigned small tasks by the pool, which it submits as shares. By joining a pool, you increase your chances of earning a small percent of a reward. If you were to solo mine, you would get to keep the whole reward for yourself, but your chances of finding a valid block solution would be next to zero.

To illustrate how hard it is to succeed as a solo miner, let's consider the total network hashrate of the Bitcoin network, which stands at about 13 exahash (EHash/s). At the same time, a good Bitcoin ASIC is only capable about 13THash/s. This means that your chances of successfully solo mining a block are one in a million, or about one block in 19 years. On top of that, the hashrate keeps increasing with the increase in the number of users. This means that it would be easier to win the lottery than to succeed as a solo miner.

However, let's assume you joined a large mining pool that provides about 25 percent of the hashrate in the network. This pool would ideally mine 25 percent of the blocks. Your 13THash/s would be equivalent to 0.0004 percent of the pool's hashrate, and you would get a similar share of the block rewards. The block reward stands at 12.5 Bitcoins, therefore you would end up with about 0.00005 BTC per block. Since your pool would ideally find about 36 blocks in a day, you would earn about 0.0018 BTC every day. With one Bitcoin currently going at about $17000, you'd get earnings of about $30 per day.

The Actual Mining

With your hardware ready and having joined a mining pool, you are now ready to start mining. All you need to do now is to download the correct software and configure it to your hardware and pool. Most mining pools will help you with instructions on where to download the software and how to configure it. It's good to note that your mining speed will be affected by things like memory, clock speeds, drivers and even firmware revisions. To get the most out of your mining software, you should check various forums for ideas on how to optimize your hardware.

One challenge that many new miners often face is deciding on the best coin to mine. This is a tricky issue because of the high price volatility in cryptocurrency prices as well as the emergence of new coins every single day. For instance, Ethereum was just another coin that was potentially profitable to mine. All of a sudden, market forces pushed its value and it became insanely profitable in no time. Switching between different coins is also a time consuming affair.

To avoid these problems, some miners use platforms such as Nicehash, WinMiner and Kryptex, which allow you to lease your hashing to others. Payments are made in Bitcoin. This transfers the burden of figuring out the best coin to mine to others and ensures you don't get stuck with some worthless coins. However, there are fees involved in this. Alternatively, you can set up a multi-algorithm mining software. Here, you create accounts for all coins you are interested in and set up rules to determine which coin will be mined at what time.

Bottom Line – Is Mining a Profitable Venture?

Before you decide to get into cryptocurrency mining, it's important to note that mining hardware does not come cheap. You should also consider the power requirements. The lower your power costs, the more likely you are to make profits from mining. Ultimately, the profitability of mining lies on the volatility that is being witnessed in the cryptocurrency market. With virtually unknown coins making over 1000% gains in a matter of months, you can easily hit the mother lode. However, it's also important to keep in mind that the price of a cryptocurrency can also plummet just as fast. Therefore, if you decide to get into cryptocurrency mining, don't risk more money than you are willing to lose.

Chapter Six:

Investing in Cryptocurrency – What You Need to Know

Since you are reading this book, I can assume that you want to learn how you can invest in cryptocurrency and make yourself some money. Following its meteoric rise, Bitcoin has created several billionaires, and you don't want to be left behind while people make insane amounts of money from this cryptocurrency craze. There are several ways of investing in cryptocurrency. The most common include buying and holding coins for speculation purposes and trading in cryptocurrencies in the same way people trade in the forex market. You could also get into mining, which we discussed in the previous chapter. In this chapter, you will learn everything you need to know about investing in cryptocurrency.

Why Invest in Cryptocurrency?

People make cryptocurrency investments for various reasons. However, there are three important reasons why you should invest in cryptocurrency. First, investing in cryptocurrency is a way of hedging your assets against the impending fall of the dollar imperium. Cryptocurrency is a wave that is silently revolutionizing money. By investing in cryptocurrency, you are essentially betting on the success of this revolution. Second, you should only invest in cryptocurrency if you support the vision behind cryptocurrency – that of universal currency that is free from control by governments. Finally, you should invest in cryptocurrencies only if you understand the technology behind them.

Unfortunately, some people are investing in cryptocurrency because of the fear of missing out (FOMO), in the hopes of making a quick buck. They don't even understand the technology. This is a very bad investment strategy.

You should also note that cryptocurrencies are not like any ordinary investment. They are more volatile than any other investment class. They are unregulated assets. They are also a very high-risk investment. There is always the risk that you could lose your key, an exchange or your wallet might get hacked, or they might even get outlawed altogether.

Building Your Portfolio – Which Cryptocurrencies Should You Buy?

For most people, the only cryptocurrency they have thought of investing in is Bitcoin. This is because up until recently, Bitcoin has been the only dominant cryptocurrency. The other altcoins have only been penny stocks with little chance of profitability. However, things have now changed. While Bitcoin remains dominant, its share in the cryptocurrency market has dropped to around 40%, down from 90%. This is mostly as a result of the growth of Ethereum as well as the scalability problems facing Bitcoin. This shows why it's important to always keep yourself abreast of any occurrences in the crypto sphere.

While Bitcoin is still a standard asset to invest in, you should balance and diversify your portfolio. Some good options to consider include Ethereum, Ripple, Dash, Litecoin, Monero and the other coins I discussed in Chapter 3. However, before you invest in a certain cryptocurrency, take your time to do your research on the coin and decide if you believe in their vision and objective. New coins are coming up each day while others are dying each day, so do your research to avoid losing your money.

Some factors you should consider before deciding on whether you want to invest in a specific cryptocurrency include:

- The transaction processing speed

- The number of coins currently in circulation

- Is the supply of coins limited or unlimited? If limited, what's the limit?

- The real-world applications of the cryptocurrency

- Real world adoption of the technology

- Background of the founders

- Does the project have any big investors?

How to Buy Your First Coins?

For beginners, the first time buying crypto coins can be confusing and challenging. Before you can buy your first coins, you need to set up your digital wallet. The issue of choosing the right cryptocurrency wallet has been covered in greater detail in Chapter 4, so I won't cover it again. Once your digital wallet is set up, the next thing is to figure out how you are going to pay for your crypto coins. Although they are also a form of money, you have to exchange them for fiat money, similar to how you would exchange your dollars for another currency when traveling abroad. The complexity of buying cryptocurrencies depends on your country's financial system, though it need not be a complicated process. Some of the methods you can use to pay for crypto coins include:

Bank transfer: This is a simple but slow way of paying for cryptocurrencies. Simply make a transfer to the seller's account and they will send you your coins the moment they receive the money. Bank transfers take about 1-2 days for the money to reflect in the seller's account, therefore you will have to wait for 1-2 days before you receive your coins.

Credit card: Despite being the most common online payment method for fiat money, it is widely unaccepted by cryptocurrency sellers. This is because with credit card payments, malicious buyers can claim chargebacks, therefore defrauding the seller. Since cryptocurrency transactions are irreversible, the seller would have no way of getting back their coins. Still, some exchanges accept credit card payments, though they charge higher prices for the cryptocurrencies.

PayPal: Just like credit cards, PayPal payments are widely unaccepted by cryptocurrency sellers because of the issue of chargebacks. Some exchanges support PayPal payments, though they also charge significantly higher prices.

Other payment channels: Different exchanges accept many other different payment methods such as Skrill, Sofort, iDEAL and many more.

Private payment channels: It's possible to pay for crypto coins through other private channels such as Western Union, Paysafecard, or using good old cash. Some p2p platforms like LocalBitcoins link buyers and sellers in the same region, allowing them to decide on their own payment methods.

Once you have figured out the best payment method for you, you can now go ahead and purchase your preferred cryptocurrency. Some common places where you can buy cryptocurrencies include exchange platforms, brokers and direct commercial exchanges, p2p markets like LocalBitcoins, through gift cards and vouchers and from cryptocurrency ATMs.

Cryptocurrency Exchanges

If your intention is to get into cryptocurrency trading, then you will definitely need to join a cryptocurrency exchange. These are platforms that allow users to exchange cryptocurrencies for fiat currencies as well as other cryptocurrencies. There are various kinds of exchanges, each meant to serve a specific kind of user. There are advanced exchanges with complex trading tools to serve professional traders, while others are there to serve people looking to make the occasional trade.

The three main types of exchanges are:

Trading platforms: These connect traders and perform the role of an escrow. They handle the processing of orders and charge fees for each transaction.

Direct trading platforms: Also referred to as p2p markets, these link buyers and sellers directly without playing the role of an intermediary. Instead of having fixed prices, they allow sellers to set their own rates.

Brokers and direct commercial exchanges: These work similar to forex brokers, exchanging cryptocurrencies for other cryptocurrencies and fiat money at fixed prices.

Factors to Consider When Choosing an Exchange

Type the words 'cryptocurrency exchange' into your browser and you will find several exchanges to choose from. With such a wide pool to choose from, you want to make sure you join a cryptocurrency exchange that best serves your needs. Some factors to keep in mind when choosing a cryptocurrency exchange include:

Reputation: Before joining, find out what other users are saying about the exchange. Read online reviews and scour cryptocurrency communities and forums.

Fees: Cryptocurrency exchanges make money by charging transaction, deposit and withdrawal fees. Find out the fee structure of an exchange before joining to avoid unanticipated charges.

Payment methods: Does the exchange support payment methods that are convenient for you? You should also keep in mind that charges will be higher for exchanges that accept PayPal and credit card payments and that bank transfers are not convenient when you need to make fast transactions.

Verification requirements: Are you looking for complete anonymity? Most exchanges will ask you for identity and proof of address documents before you can start trading. Are you willing to provide this information?

Geographical restrictions: Does the exchange offer full support in your geographic region?

Exchange rates: Cryptocurrency exchanges also make profits from their spreads. Check their rates and spreads to ensure you are getting the best deal.

Evaluating an exchange based on the above considerations will ensure that you join a cryptocurrency exchange that is best suited to your needs. Some popular cryptocurrency exchanges that you might consider include Coinbase, Kraken, Poloniex, Shapeshift and LocalBitcoins.

When Should You Buy?

If you listen to cryptocurrency traders, you will hear them talking about good and bad times to buy. So, when is the best time to buy? There is no rule of the thumb as to when you should buy cryptocurrencies. However, you should avoid buying at the peak of a bubble. Neither should you buy when prices are crashing. As the trader's saying goes, 'Never catch a falling knife'. The best times to buy are when prices are relatively low and stable.

To be a successful trader, you need to learn how to determine when a bubble is about to burst and when the price hits the bottom after falling. However, no one can predict this with ultimate certainty. For instance, when Bitcoin rose to $1000, many people were afraid of buying, thinking that this was the peak of the bubble. The price rose to $10000 and many more thought that this must certainly be the peak. However, Bitcoin defied their prediction and continued rising, nearly hitting the $20000 mark. You should also avoid comparing cryptocurrency bubbles to financial bubbles, since cryptocurrencies are highly volatile.

Risks of Cryptocurrency Investing/Trading

Despite some people having become instant millionaires and billionaires through cryptocurrency investing and trading, this does not mean that there are no risks in it. Here are some risks you face when you decide to become a cryptocurrency investor.

Some technologies will fail: You should keep in mind that cryptocurrencies are basically software or lines of code. Remember the dot.com bust? Some cryptocurrencies will fail in the same way that some software companies failed in the dot.com era. Back in the '90s, there was a lot of hype about the new thing known as the internet, which promised to change the world. Well, the internet did change the world. It created overnight billionaires. However, a lot of people also lost their money there as well. The same thing will happen with cryptocurrency. By investing in a cryptocurrency, you are simply betting on that software. Some will change the world and create immense wealth, while others will fade from the face of the earth. Learn to differentiate winners from losers.

It requires technical savvy: Cryptocurrencies were developed by super-geeks, and to most people, cryptocurrencies are still geeky. To get into cryptocurrency, you need to be good with computers. At least until more user-friendly cryptocurrency interfaces are built. Why am I saying this? With cryptocurrencies, you are dealing with cash. You need to be well-versed with various aspects of computer and internet security. Otherwise, you might wake up to find a zero balance on your digital wallet. You also need to understand the basics of how cryptocurrencies work to enable you bet on those with the highest chance of success.

Broker and technology risk: Cryptocurrency is still in its infancy, therefore there are still lots of unknowns. Many things could change. New security vulnerabilities might emerge. Remember how millions of traders lost their money after the hacking of MtGox? If anything, you should consider dealing with cryptocurrency brokers to be about twice as risky as dealing with forex brokers.

Factors That Affect the Price of A Cryptocurrency

Cryptocurrency prices are affected by several factors, sometimes leading to very abrupt changes. Some factors you need to keep in mind include:

Exchange listing: This is a major mover of cryptocurrency prices. Whenever a large cryptocurrency exchange announces that they will start listing a certain cryptocurrency, you can expect the price to shoot in the near future.

Software upgrades: Cryptocurrencies undergo software upgrades either to solve existing challenges in the network or to improve functionality. For example, there was a hotly debated argument about making a software upgrade to improve Bitcoin's transaction processing speed. This argument ended with the split of Bitcoin Cash from Bitcoin. Watch out for software upgrades since they are highly likely to affect the price of a cryptocurrency.

Public hype: Just like company stocks, cryptocurrency prices can be affected by fake news.

Wallet improvements: Some investors buy cryptocurrencies and hold them for a couple years as they wait for prices to rise. Therefore, storage is an important part of the cryptocurrency equation. In their initial stages, most cryptocurrencies are still geeky, with wallets that are not beginner-friendly. This keeps the non-techie investors from these cryptocurrencies. Therefore, cryptocurrencies without good wallets are often undervalued. Introduction of a better, user-friendly wallet opens these cryptocurrencies to the masses and therefore often leads to an increase in price.

Platform applications: Some cryptocurrency platforms are more than digital currencies. For instance, Ethereum is a platform that allows the building and deployment of other applications. If one of the applications built on a cryptocurrency platform does well, it can lead to an increase in the value of the underlying platform. Therefore, it's good to watch out for any promising apps that are hosted on the cryptocurrency platform you are trading in.

Government regulation: Government policies also have an effect on the effect of cryptocurrencies. For instance, Bitcoin prices fell before rebounding in September 2017 after China announced that it had banned cryptocurrency trading in the country. You should keep abreast of any government policy trends and avoid cryptocurrencies that are likely to be red flagged by governments.

Chapter Seven:

The Future of Cryptocurrency

2017 has been a big year for cryptocurrency. Many cryptocurrencies saw a lot of growth, with some like Bitcoin, Bitcoin Cash, Dash and Ethereum seeing exponential growth. As we move forward, the crypto space will only keep growing. According to some industry experts, the coming year will see mass public awareness for cryptocurrencies. Here are some of the things expected to happen in the crypto world within the next one year.

Taxation Will Become A Huge Issue

While many people have made massive wealth in the cryptocurrency market, many have been keeping their away from the eyes of the government. In the coming one year, you can expect that the IRS will be more focused on clamping down on cryptocurrency investors to make sure they pay their taxes.

Number of Users Will Rise

There is no doubt that the number of cryptocurrency users is going to increase in the next one year. As public awareness of cryptocurrencies grows and as the software becomes more user-friendly to non-techies, you can bet that there will be increased uptake of cryptocurrencies. Some industry experts predict that in the next one year, more than 50 million people will hold at least one cryptocurrency.

Bitcoin to Develop into A Payment Network

Though it was meant to be an electronic payments system, many people currently consider Bitcoin as a store of value and a speculative asset. However, according to Trevor Koverko, CEO of a cryptocurrency technology company, Bitcoin's utility and price will increase dramatically, leading to its emergence as a fully-fledged payment network. This will be driven by the emergence of scaling solutions such as Lighting Network. However, for Bitcoin to become a fully-fledged payment network, its community needs to be willing to adopt these upgrades.

Cryptocurrencies Are Here to Stay

To some people, cryptocurrencies are a passing fad, something that will lose momentum as fast as it gained. However, industry experts believe that cryptocurrencies and the blockchain technology are here to stay. Some platforms like NEO and Ethereum will push the adoption of the technology since they help people create blockchain applications that have meaningful uses in the real world. The adoption of these real world applications by the corporate world will increase the demand for cryptocurrencies and therefore ensure their longevity.

Diversification of Assets by Investors

Currently, most investors hold their assets in Bitcoin and Ethereum. However, you can expect that more people will start diversifying their portfolios into other cryptocurrencies like

Dash, Litecoin, IOTA, NEM and many more. Many investors will diversify their crypto-assets in much the same way that they approach other traditional assets. Many more cryptocurrencies will also come up in the coming year. Some will be introduced to tackle the challenges being experienced by existing cryptocurrencies while others will introduce new niches altogether. There is a high likelihood that some of the new cryptocurrencies will become very profitable.

Increased Interest from Institutional Investors

Up until recently, institutional investors have been looking at cryptocurrency with a very skeptical eye. However, the year 2017 has seen the entry of some big name institutions into the industry. According to The Crypto Company CEO Mike Poutre, the coming year will see decreased volatility in the price of Bitcoin, which will in turn attract more institutional investors and lead to the growth of alternative cryptocurrencies. Mike even predicts that the increased interest from institutional investors might push the market cap of the cryptocurrency industry past the $5 trillion mark in the next one year.

Increased Regulation

Currently, many countries do not have any policies in regards to cryptocurrencies. However, several governments have been keenly watching their usage and growth. As more people adopt cryptocurrencies, governments will start putting in place regulations surrounding their use. Some financial institutions like Barclays Bank are also trying to push for the adoption of cryptocurrencies and the blockchain technology into the conventional financial system. ICOs are most likely to be the first area to be affected by regulation, before it moves on to the cryptocurrencies themselves. Most regulations might also seek to promote the adoption of KYC (Know Your Customer) laws in order to track the flow of funds and improve transparency. While it is impossible to predict the impact of regulation on cryptocurrencies, there is a high likelihood that regulation will not hinder their growth.

Cryptocurrencies Will Force Conventional Financial Systems to Level Up

Currently, banks and traditional payment processors are enjoying extremely high transaction fees. They are also very slow, with most international transactions being processed in 1-3 days. Cryptocurrencies, on the other hand, are very fast and have extremely low processing fees. These advantages might push more businesses to cryptocurrencies. If they are to remain relevant, banks and traditional payment processors will need to up their game.

Conclusion

Despite still being in its infancy stage, cryptocurrency is silently and steadily revolutionizing the world, particularly the financial and investment sector. Due to the many advantages offered by cryptocurrency, many businesses and individuals are gradually starting to accept it. Many investors have also switched from traditional investment assets to crypto-assets. In the last 2 years, the industry has also created many overnight millionaires and billionaires. Since the industry is still in its initial stages, we can expect that there will be some challenges and hurdles to be overcome before it achieves mainstream adoption. However, we can be certain that the cryptocurrency industry will be the next revolution in the world as we know it. This shows why it is important to jump into the cryptocurrency train before it leaves the station and you miss out. Having reached the end of this book, I hope that you will use the knowledge learned in this book to get into the world of cryptocurrency and build a fortune for yourself.

www.ingramcontent.com/pod-product-compliance
Lightning Source LLC
Chambersburg PA
CBHW071233220526
45468CB00002B/828